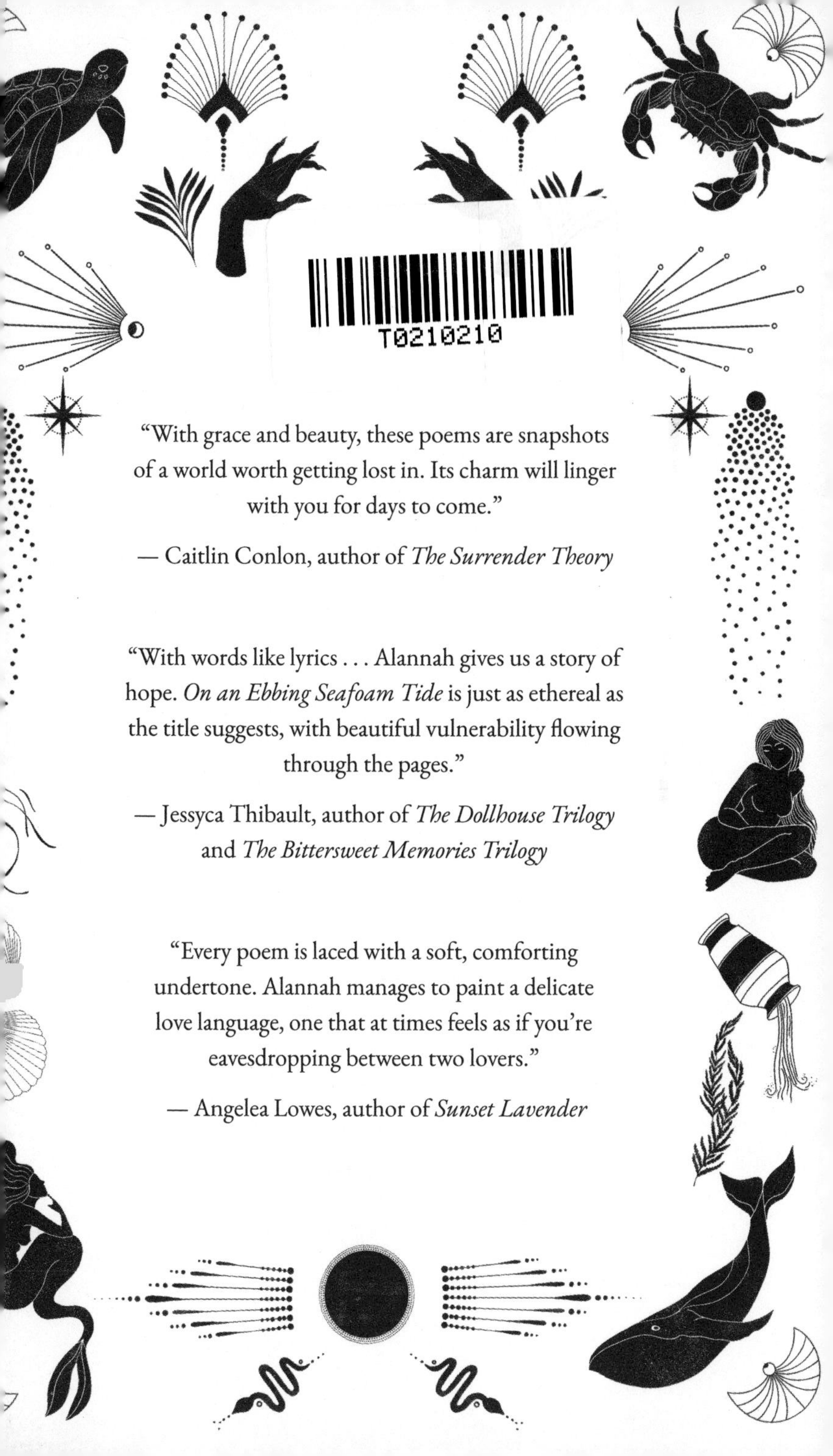

"With grace and beauty, these poems are snapshots of a world worth getting lost in. Its charm will linger with you for days to come."

— Caitlin Conlon, author of *The Surrender Theory*

"With words like lyrics . . . Alannah gives us a story of hope. *On an Ebbing Seafoam Tide* is just as ethereal as the title suggests, with beautiful vulnerability flowing through the pages."

— Jessyca Thibault, author of *The Dollhouse Trilogy* and *The Bittersweet Memories Trilogy*

"Every poem is laced with a soft, comforting undertone. Alannah manages to paint a delicate love language, one that at times feels as if you're eavesdropping between two lovers."

— Angelea Lowes, author of *Sunset Lavender*

ON AN EBBING SEAFOAM TIDE

alannah radburn

2023

Note: the poem on page 26 was written using a prompt from Rupi Kaur via Instagram

Published by Central Avenue Publishing, an imprint of Central Avenue Marketing Ltd.
www.centralavenuepublishing.com

ON AN EBBING SEAFOAM TIDE

Trade Paperback: 978-1-77168-293-0
Epub: 978-1-77168-294-7

Published in Canada
Printed in United States of America

1. POETRY / Women Authors   2. POETRY / LGBT

10 9 8 7 6 5 4 3 2 1

Keep up with Central Avenue

for chantal,

my oceans boil down to you:

the final line.
of the last poem.
i'll ever write.

Foreword

Great poetry requires three things—originality, figurative language, and a clear voice. As a poet and author myself, this is something I think about often. You see, just because something is catchy or affirmative doesn't make it poetry. A metaphor can be clever, but if it isn't original, I file it under recycled noise. And being able to conjure beautiful, original lines laden with metaphor still doesn't make good poetry if the lines lack voice, if they lack a good story. My favorite thing about Alannah Radburn? She has managed to master all three.

I fell in love with Radburn's writing when I read her first collection, *Yellow*, back in 2018. I've read it more times than I can count, and its pages are well-loved and marked up like an old college textbook. One of my favorite lines of poetry lies within its pages (our hands interlocked; fingers weaved like baskets) from a poem called "As Simple As Hand Holding." Not only do I find Radburn's writing to be original and beautiful (sometimes heartbreakingly so), I also find it to be filled with meaning, especially for me—and hopefully for you, too.

Alannah is a self-described queer poet and feminist, which is reflected constantly in her work. She paints the intersection of queer love and femininity in the most astounding light, and I would be surprised if I am the only queer woman she's helped empower to be her truest self. Radburn uses her platform and voice not only to convey magic in the form of words, but also to expose her readers to less conventional love stories, which too often are portrayed as toxic and destructive in the media, or worse, are not portrayed at all.

Alongside Alannah's other books, *On an Ebbing Seafoam Tide* calls my bookshelf home. This collection explores a queer relationship in the most intimate light, and love and heartbreak in a way that will form a beautiful, longing ache below your sternum long after you finish reading. It will bring affirmation and solidarity to anyone currently in love, and comfort and hope to anyone who's recently lost someone. Whether you are yearning for love or already in its warm embrace, you'll feel right at home here.

My hope is that as you hold this book in your hands, you'll find as much brilliance in its pages as I do.

xx, Emily Juniper

contents

what do you see in this ocean glass?

is it soft or monstrous,

sand or shark?

do the whitecaps scare you,

or do you long for the pull of a riptide;

anything that mirrors what you already know—

what is calm one moment,

brings calamity in the next breath.

SEABREEZE

my waterfall lover shows me the scars on her hands,
the rivers in her hair,
the soul inside my body.

my waterfall lover's heart falls out her mouth in similar fashion;
plunging to unseeable depths.

my waterfall lover looks me in the eyes and
suddenly
i'm the one in the barrel,

toppling right over the edge.

the sun is reflected
in the apples of her eyes;
swaying from a tree under which i lay daily.
the cardinals spiral red,
the sun sets eternal,

the fruit is ripe as summer.

you gift me your laughter
and it is wrapped in sunlight;
which is to say
it's the only warm thing i've known all my life,

and i wouldn't mind if it swallowed me whole one day.

red velvet slips down the back of my throat
like a shadow out the side door.
i'm quietly watching my temptress
as she tips her glass backward, merging with the bloodred clouds.
she flows freely like our cabernet;
a slow burn,
a sweet venom that starts in the ankle,
killing every molecule of doubt
on its way up to the chest.
on its way to stop my beating heart in its tracks.
her tongue is red,
and raw
like tastebuds lost to a scalding wave.
you can burn me, love.
lap like a dying cat on its ninth life at a desert oasis.
for you, water is in abundance.

for you, oceans run wild.

i remember the days of writing tattered love letters
on a grooved, oak table of an old bar,
sticky with the remnants of hasty decisions.
snippets of conversation
dance with the flames in mason jars.

the stars smile wide-mouthed grins;
cheshire cat constellations.
laughter emanates from the depths of bellies,
soars to the sky like kite-string thoughts.
smells and sounds snag memories,
yank them up the wells of yesterday.

how the evergreen in my eyes opens for you.

her compassion, a gentle breeze,
delicately lifts the hair from my shoulders
to kiss the softness of my wound.
in this dreamy seascape of a moment, i realize
that never in my life
have i been spoken to in a love language such as this

and yet i understand every word.

candles glow in the hollowed-out tree;
the leaves rustle,
branches whisper in the language of the wind,
passing messages along the deep navy of the sky.

thoughts scatter like seeds,
take to the soil.
the inescapable chill of impending dark thrills.
it's electric.
the candles flicker

but they never go out.

a lone firework splits the sky in two
as the warm wind's temper shifts—
docile to wild.
can you tell someone you love them with your gaze
long before she's ready to hear it?
the sandy earth is moving underfoot,
but her arm sits steady on my shoulders.
love is a volatile ocean,
and i dare not count the times i've been cautioned:

you can't keep diving in wide open
and be surprised when you come up with salt in your eyes.

but i love the thrill of a current,
and a little salt keeps me alive.
the sky thunders once again, and a blast of light
reflects her eyes into mine.

yep.

fireworks.

actually,

forget fireworks.

i drift to reverie;
to be the one who knows what kind of herbal tea
she sips at night,
the one that knows that specific sound her espresso machine makes
right before you need to take it off the heat.
her shower runs hot,
and it's always cool in her bedroom.
i want to know her rainy days and grocery store lists,
the brand of shampoo she uses.
to know her mundane is to be
gifted her intimacy.
anyone can light a match, explode passion into the sky;
anyone can put on a show.
but only her sweetest love
is given opportunity to witness the stillness,

the everyday dance of her truest being.

i handed you a fistful of honesty
perched upon an upturned palm
topped with ripe berries;
the red running like watercolour
down my skin—
but this time,
it didn't remind me of blood.
you eyed this display of openness,
gaze carved with affection.
you split your soft, sweet strawberry mouth,

and devoured it whole.

the bathwater isn't even warm anymore,
i just want to sit in the element.
thinking of past beaches,
revelations and sand.
what has the life sea taken from you?
i once hung twilight curtains from the rafters, invited in the bats.
living in a night snowglobe;
shake it.
stars drift on lukewarm bathwater

and settle at my feet.

she balances ornamental teacups
atop her brow,
writes poems on my skin.
along my thighs
she whispers words of endless origin.
there's flour on her nose;
          footsteps soft,
she's been baking
in the hardwood kitchen again.
the sun streaks her flyaway hairs,
flowery music slips from her lips
and softly garnishes my anticipation.
in these moments i know
how to tumble deep down,
to worship the very ground under her feet.
but instead,
like the dough she kneads,

i'll rise to the occasion.

i'm busy crossing the street and

she's busy crossing my mind—
where all roads meet,
and all lights are green

and all signs point to her.

it's the first week of spring,
and i feel you in everything.

crocus, daisy, afternoon rays;
the kettle is about to boil.
the light is climbing like vines.
my chest rises and falls in time with the earth,
and you, my sweet sun,
have pushed air into these tired lungs;
have swept winter under doors and rugs,
have planted gardens with me.
i hold this so delicately in my hands.
i have the power to open like a flower
and remember
lazy daydreams of all the bloomings that led to us.
back to the days of butterfly nets,
and a carefree meadow by my grandmother's lake;
swinging
and coming up with clouds of coloured wings.
how my soft, childlike petals have changed,
into fields of unyielding sunflowers.

just in time for you to come wandering by,
with a fondness for yellow blossoms,
and a yearning curiosity for a life
that is sweet,
boundless,

and waiting to be ours.

there are over 200 bones inside of me,
packed with marrow.
all this life
teeming under my skin.
this body is an ecosystem,

and i am the creator.

there is ivy in your hair as you climb from the swamp,
evergreen eyes skyward.
hold your heart outside the body and offer it up to the
forest in sacrifice;
it is only human. frail and replaceable.
necks can snap like twigs
but the marsh-fire inside you

is not so easily snuffed.

her hair smells of campfire and
frenzied devotion;
            she looks at me like i'm in trouble.
like i've lived here all my life.

summer is growing around us like weeds,
like we've never sipped cold inhibition
            even once before.
she storms right up to the windows of august
and throws them outward,
along with any decency we may have had:

we have no use for it here.

a small harvest nymph
eats berries and watches the sun set
while perched atop a toadstool.
the soup is coming to a rolling boil over the coals
in the small of the tree trunk.

life is simple, really.

ask me why i love you;
ask the desert if she feels time.
a human heartbeat, a geological blink.
            we exist when the eyes are closed,
the darkness a backdrop to two starlit silhouettes.
this place is only us.
            a geological eternity.
soft sailing across the inner lid,
rippling moonshine. oceans hang heavy in the air.
only forever.

only horizons.

after the fight:

even our rainiest, stormiest days
run down the window pane,
pooling in a well at the bottom.
it is here that we dip our brushes,
paint life into our dried-out watercolours.

hot air balloon skies; violet backdrops.
rose-pink cheeks splash across the horizon,
blending our sunsets together.

we float gently through this life,
knowing that each storm we weather
paints our coming vistas more vibrantly.

our complexities make love to our skylines,
the monsoons water our colours and give us
limitless potential.
this is how we turn anger into art.

this is how we've made a masterpiece of us.

do the
evergreen treetops
revisit
whatever happened to them
while they were hugging the soil,
or are they now anchored to the soaring breeze;
the past beneath them,
a mere whisper in ancient roots.

a small echo in a forgotten chamber.

closure.

IN MY EDEN,
THERE IS NO ADAM.

when we met,
we were standing on the edge of spring,
looking down into summer.

the days grew longer,
the sky filled with shooting stars;
that's august for you.
each time i saw one drop from the sky behind her,
i made the same wish.
and to this lucky day,

i'm still burning up in her atmosphere.

here lies

the living home.

she has deep roots and stretches past the clouds. a castle in the sky. the pulse beats in windows and in spires.

the door is the wide, wide trunk of a tree. you enter straight into her heart. whether she lets you in; the tree decides.

the bricks are laid halfway up. stones in the upper branches. she's ancient; she is nature.

no neighbours within a stone's throw. property is yours. the grove, the vale, the meadow, the heart of the forest; the air is fresh.

the doorbell sings. swims through the caverns like a soft awakening. a comforting toll. mythic—you'll feel it in your depths.

the wood. it's smooth. polished. rustic.

the staircase climbs and spirals to meet the stones of the skyward castle. it's open. it's warm and wide. there's always natural light.

get into the roots. tunnels, bookcases disguising more tunnels. stone labyrinths, shadows and vaults. it smells of cedar. of wet, deep forest.

there is warmth in the kitchen. there is something in the oven, there is family round the isle. dragon fire ignites the stove. flour dusts the slate.

then there's the library. she's a thousand years old and bursting with poetry. the smell of books, the quickening of flipped pages, the glow of kerosene.

do you taste salt yet?

do you see keys and tapestries?

do you feel her spell?

she changes herself. self-sustaining. old bricks are eaten by the wood; they form something anciently new.
each day, she's different in small ways, but the core stays stable. the trunk holds mystery.
when you leave, you won't know how much time has passed. you feel like you've stepped out of something completely arcane.
laughter still echoes in your mind. the house grows steady.
the magic builds. you will be left with a dire longing to return.
remember,

you can always come home.

PULLING TIDES

a relationship is perched on the windowsill,
delicate as a tomato.
here is where the problem lies:
one person believes it is ripening
while

the other person believes it is rotting.

is it an intrusive thought or is it intuition?
should i listen intently or should i file it away,
to wherever all the thoughts float?
how to tell the difference;
what is a warning, what is a farce?
decoding one's own brain—
sometimes it would seem easier to pick the locks at the louvre,
bet i could even crack a smile on mona lisa,
telling her all the things my mind tries to trick me into thinking.
she would tell me that
half the people who see her think that she is scheming,
half think she is deep in thought,
and a third half think her upset.
someone even told her to get bangs;
but the truth belongs to her alone.
'back to your thoughts' she tells me.
does anyone know your truth deeper than you?
has anyone else visited the caves in those oceans?
it is from there your veins carry that intuition to the heart.

trust yourself.

i saw a spider in the corner of my mind yesterday
and today it is not there.
i find myself ambiently nervous, wondering where it is now.
what part of the room is it hiding in,

where will it show up?

they're setting us up.
eve whispers to lilith, fruit ripe in hand.

they want to use us as a reason to persecute women;
we're the original witches.

their laughter lilts through fields of flowers,
parting clouds of butterfly wings like nectared breath.

you know, lilith sighs,
they say the white flowers of queen anne's lace represent sanctuary.
the way you wear them makes me want to transgress.

eve bites the apple.

there. we're sinners now, dear. what else have we to lose?

her flowers fall to the earth,

exposing all places truly holy.

the night tugs wildly at her hair,
the wind whips it;
          twenty lashes
of freedom.
wicked smiles paint the sky,
composing a masterpiece on her constellations.
the music she sings is quick as nightfall,
indulgent as this thick plum obscurity

within which the women run.

sometimes, i feel like i want more than anyone can ever give me.
i'm a three-headed baby bird in the nest
screaming, beaks wide, straining open,

tendons threatening to break.

there are studies showing that baby sea turtles are attracted to the horizon light. this guides them instinctually towards the ocean;
towards safety and freedom and that big blue expanse where
everything is going to happen.

they also say that female sea turtles return to the same beach on which they were born to lay their own eggs. they cross several hundreds of kilometers of open ocean with no landmarks pointing them home, and make it there anyways.

oceanography experts.

i don't think science really understands it, but anyone who's been in love might.
you get it, right? how you could find your way back to them in any endless night? over any distance. across everlasting oceans.

you just close your eyes and feel the water around you. bending beneath you, sliding across you, whispering to you and gently tugging you in their direction. an indigo wishing well, asking for nothing and granting each wave in return. feeling her on all currents.
landmarks or water. this is how i'll always find my love; just as the sea turtles find their first beach. i'll look deep into her eyes and see it: that big blue expanse,
where everything is going to happen.

that horizon light pointing me home.

a damp towel slowly draws the salt down her skin,
dewdrops of empathy rise.
serpentine coils of steam whisper blushing words in the candlelight.
the spine delicately rises out of the body and twists with song.
  a pulsing rosette.
burning words of velvet compassion drape the vertebrae.
you wish to hold her regal backbone
in your human hands.
there is nothing but truth here.

nothing but murmurs of great genesis.

you know the saying about the tree and the wooden axe.

i remember everything that i have done to myself.

early november brings with it
colder weather and faded-to-grey thoughts of you.
all this rain on my upturned palms, all this sorrow
dipping its hands into me and licking its fingers dry.
      i am still,
feeling with an immensity that could drown oceans.
i don't know where all the thoughts go,
do they drift off to some invisible place,
somewhere in the atmosphere?
is there a timeless whirlpool
of everything anyone has ever thought of me?
would it make me weep;

      would it make me proud?

it is a knowing.
a depth of feeling, a certitude.
her eyelashes. the sunshine on her face.
it is a boat gliding through waters. the green in her eyes. it is the roots of creation.
the tabletop at the last supper, desperate to be eaten off of.
it is sacrifice that doesn't feel like sacrifice. greedy and hungry, shy and reserved.

sometimes it doesn't know when
to stop playing hide and seek, to show itself the light of day,
the dreamdance of moon.
it is butterfly wings drying on a buttercup,
a young girl rescuing a helpless thing.
doing the dishes with a full heart, making her side of the bed
and making up with each other. forgiving myself for the brutality i've bestowed;
on myself and on others.
it's a superhero movie that evokes empathy for the villain. our origin story.
everything in between. it is her.
it is me.
the capacity in my heart,

despite all i've lived through.

i think your smile still knows its way around here;
knows exactly where to curve,
how to slip its way right through the bolts of my front door;

lockpicker.

YOU EXPOSE ME
LIKE A NERVE
ENDING.

actions speak louder than words,
but the way you make me feel

is a scream more deafening than both of them.

teacups clink together;
honey rolls over the brim of the china.
we dance under petals, dewdrops falling like rain;
painting small paths down the leaves.
leaving them striped like peppermint candies.
just when i think i've lost my magic,
she returns in full force.
the night is a flower;
its sunlessness smells of unending

opportunity.

they turned the dull, metallic taste of blood
into something shimmering
            and kind.
my dear alchemists,
thank you.

family.

beside the ancient rose garden
tunneled deep into the soft earth
is a woman whose cutlass has been taken.
she is pliable, cotton spine;
    fleshy rage.
the roses feed from her earthly energy
petals shaping the mountainside,
thorns carving the canyons.
her small, round mass of skin
is pulsing with life
    and with each turn of the earth
she rampantly searches for those who stole from her.
it is from here that her fingertips encircle the globe
and the necks of each
who claimed her blade as their own.
you cannot take from the matriarchy of the planet
and expect an obedient landscape underfoot.

traitors

her gaze so tender,
it turns stone to flesh;

fossil to skin.

we slip into the night
like a woman into a silk evening dress;

softly.
exquisitely.

it is moments before an ocean sweet sundown.
head thrown all the way back,
hazy blues
enter the greens of my eyes.
there is a certain palatability to the air
enough to fill my lungs with salt
as warm car exhaust ruffles my hair;

i can taste the volatile freedom.

a vacant seashell,
an empty home,
can roar into your ear
and claim to be the ocean.

no wonder i mistook you as a force of nature.
something so hollow
can be wildly enticing;
can claim the waves and the whitecaps as their own

all the while remaining devoid of substance,
deserted as an idle ghost town,

sunken as a shipwreck.

it was an earl grey morning;
the sands bled and wept
and the ocean sang its melodic tune.

the wings of this aircraft
bent under the sadness
of carrying me far,

far away from you.

pay close attention;
her eyes are huntresses.
she can shoot daggers across a room.

across a whole country.

the butterfly effect never would have come into reality
if the caterpillar hadn't escaped its cocoon.
what do you call it if something happened before the chain reaction?
if it never flapped its wings in the first place,
the butterfly effects itself out of existence;

leaving you in full control.

young eyes regard the grandmother
crush the dead part of the plant in her hand.

it's called pruning,
she says
to a youthfully confused gaze;
unable to comprehend that
removal can be synonymous with growth.
as an adult,
small lessons become more clear.
cutting away the unwanted;
welcoming more fruitful flowers,
shaping new success—
it all starts by closing a strong, decisive fist
around the dead parts
that no longer serve.

weeding.

i observe my thoughts, like the therapists say;
like i'm on a train,
landscapes of my inner worlds sweeping by at great speed.

to be behind this pane of glass;
tea clasped in hand.
to hear the sound of a crisp page turning and turning;
new horizons.

to pay no mind to the thoughts outside the window;
to the clouds rolling in on the skyline.

to the hell-storm brewing in the distance.

OCEAN BLUES

the moonflower blooms only under the
quiet, silk fabric of the night.
ethereal and plush, a pastel lemon scent;
she is poison.
enticing those curious enough
to desire such deadly elegance.
to dance with a drowned man,
to whisper sweet nothings to the devil,
to watch the moon weep into her own reflection on the waves,
it keeps you alive just long enough

to feel you slip into the night's eternal embrace.

i am a woman of two bodies:

one survived the initial scream.

the other houses the echoes.

you must have hired a damn good ghostwriter
to compose all those grandiose speeches of yours.
melodrama loses its footing and slips from your mouth
like some mythic waterfall of deceit.
i don't care for the words;

you need to show me you've changed.

if he was a promise,
i was a schoolgirl linking pinkies:

vowing to never let go.

despite the ambered preservation of my recollections,
he's no longer the young child who visits my deepest dreams;
flower in hand to tuck behind my ear,
sunbeam in his pocket.

somewhere by the ocean, he is growing up;
making friends and going to school.
i'm nothing more than a weathered memory
lost to the currents.
a heart on a sleeve that became unbuttoned,
leaving the small organ to wash away to sea;

like a message in a bottle

that no one will ever read.

silence may be one of the deadliest things in the animal kingdom;

birdsong stops when a predator is near,
crickets hush when killers are loose;
the closer the danger, the quieter it gets.

so when he tells you this is our secret
that is your cue—

grab the megaphone/run as fast as you can.

you pick out girls like you're going to the pet shop—

glass windows
glass ceilings
lit by the gaslight.
you come out at night and scavenge:

this one's got good eyes.
look at the pout on that one.

people like you dangle fruit in front of our faces,
and think it disgusting when we bite.
the apple doesn't fall far from the abuser;
seeds of pure poison.

in all your density, our overarching secret has yet to be discovered.
the antidote is our teeth:

vengeful and snapping.

YOU RUN FROM
THE TRUTH FASTER
THAN A STALLION
IN PURSUIT OF
FREEDOM.

the sky is falling;
and it doesn't have a parachute.
to plummet from oneself,
to lose oneself;

is death in its most intimate form.

old wounds
are like a worn and folded paper,
stretched and smoothed on the desk countless times.
they crease;
and with the smallest touch or pressure,
fold right back into their previous shape.
such is the game of neurons,
of ancient pain.
once you've been bent a certain way,
there remains a delicate weakness,

an origami of past lives.

deep in your chest,
an unsolvable cave system.
you do not need its tangibility to prove what happened.
the human loved you,
the human is gone.
let the air take the burden,
scatter it thin over wide, vast prairies.
release your organs,
your visceral ties.

you are free to go.

he was a magician;
put my mind into a hat

and made it disappear.

he'd sharpen his tongue
and hold it to my throat;
a slick blade starved for blood.
don't tell me words are not
the most powerful thing in this world;

they've doubtlessly completed the most beheadings.

it was hard to believe in justice
when the questions they asked had me sifting through my truth,
    my horror history
up to my elbows in past misery,
machete in hand, cutting through the jungles of sick,
sick depression.

in front of the investigator he plays it off as a casual mistake,
he plays it off as if the girl wasn't so,
    so young,
staring straight into the jaws of hell.
he plays it off as if he wasn't the hellfire,
plays it off like a game;

    and i've never been good at games.

it was hard to believe in the justice
when they tried to preserve his reputation
like canned peaches at christmas time,
when they tried to pretend
that he didn't change the course of my entire
    everything.

prove what he did,
and prove it again.
your word against his authority
your witnesses against his prestige
your credibility against his influence
your strength against his manipulation.

it was hard to believe in the justice
when the justice
mounted the heads of women like me

along the wall like trophies.

it was hard to believe in anything;
so i took up the hunt,
mounted his head in the hall,

and won.

the truth is much less frightening in a poem.
it's not as scary to see a dead body,
call it art

when it's in a museum.

there is a certain beauty in unraveling;
you're left with ample loose thread

to stitch new opportunities.

that late night phone light;
eyes sweeping back and forth,
fingers traveling faster than
the thoughts that are racing:
        it's a relay and the baton is spinning
and spinning
and twisting into
the screen.
the partition between worlds;
what is real and here

        and what is everywhere.

the body knows when something is not okay;
when the bad ones try to quietly pickpocket your sanity.
they tell women that it's not all men,

but when you walk through a meadow of safety
and catch poison ivy,
you don't see the flowers rising in protest.

why are the flowers never rising in protest?

not everything is metaphor
sometimes it's just friendship
and showing up every day with a joke to tell
a warm hug to gift
a straightforward
loving
embrace

a perfect cup of tea.

i know that i paint people i love in their best colours;
my eyes have always been trained to see
the good that comes rushing at me,
to open my arms so wide to it that
even if they break,
    i'd still call the fractures beautiful.

you're the first thing i'd rescue in a fire—
even if the pedestal i've placed you upon burns.

even if your colours start to run dark.

it doesn't even have time to become history
before it repeats itself.
all of the lawmakers and pocket-liners
slide on their sunglasses
and try to sneak out the exit wounds
in the back.
but the rest of the world sees you;

and the rest of the world will plant flowers
and mourn for the children.

while america loads another gun.

nothing can harbour this sadness.

she is too big a ship.

are these explosives in my hands;
another fistful of hardened words
to throw at the person i love.

civility, caught on my nails, rips right off in the backswing.
all that's left are bloodied fingers grasping at any compassion
that surely exists somewhere inside of me
below all this heated emotion
that i've tried and failed to tame
again,
and again,

and again.

the reactive brain is not the villain;
the shadow is a part of you.
it is an old sore,
it is an open bruise.

if you send the pain to its room
it will keep coming back, hostile and howling.

talk to it. soothe it like you would a child.
it's okay to have reactions,
            it's okay to have an open wound.
your wiser self can speak kindly to this other part of yourself,
and it may be vital that you do so.

self compassion.

i dropped my baby teeth without a second thought;
i bleed for a week straight every month.
i am not afraid to take off parts of myself
    for anything.
i'll shed like a fucking dog
if it means you'll find remnants of me

lifetimes later.

you’ve never been lucky,
but have defied the odds countless times.
            is that the same thing?

hardship luck:
a rabbit’s foot, but
only if you go hunt, kill, and skin it yourself.
            maybe it’s better that way
not to wish for good fortune–

but to mould it with your bare hands.

years had passed interpreting the abuse as lullaby.
how do you retrain the mind,
after eons of sleeping through it—

alarm bells pounding on unwilling ears.

open your eyes to the downpour.
leaving isn't easy, but rather
a necessary, drenching gift.
when was the last time you gifted yourself freedom?
have you ever adorned yourself in opportunity?

the silent death march will dismantle your bones,
shred you raw,
leave you gleaming in the midsummer rain.
such strength is a birthright.

such pure vulnerability is glory.

SALT SPRAY

the wind is drying my sea hair
as i sip a pilsner under the hot atlantic sun.

i think i will be okay
without your
tepid
pacific

love.

small town is tucked under the arm of a mountain;
kind grandmother
arbouring her young.
he cliff stood next to me
egal and windswept,
ike a dashing equestrian boy.
late water drops spray the rocks below.
narled tree trunks are the pillars of this place.
veryone's secrets are much
ike the fog;
minous at first,
hen spreading themselves so thin,

they disappear entirely.

the tea steaming on the counter,
the soft picnic blankets hang on the line.
cicadas sing a warm welcome to this comfort:
        to being home

        to hearing the whitecaps crash in the blue.

i saw a leaf drift past the window
and wondered where it was off to.
important shopping to do,
a party to attend,
a river to sullenly fall into

and simply be carried away.

DO NOT BACK THE
FERAL ANIMAL OF
YOUR SADNESS INTO
A CORNER.

september graces the rising sky
as the dirt begins to settle.
the swaying night train is
approaching a station in the distance
where it will rest a while.
soft waters of poetry flow freely
along the soil this time of year,
releasing bouquets of perfumed
forest, earth and clay
to the air;
all spiced with hope.
summery hands slip together to keep warm
in this new shivery landscape.
they don't let go;

even when warmer weather returns.

what of the view beyond these hotel room curtains?

if it isn't those grey-green,
ash-blue,
lake-in-the-middle-of-august eyes,

i can't see any reason to pull back the blinds.

the stars came to rest on the collar of her jacket,
she brushes them off in the snow.
fluttering away like quiet siren song
the wind sighs them along;
snowflake,
after snowflake,
after snowflake,

before delight.

there are plants growing out of teacups;
the bookshelf is full, and the books,
much like dandelions,
have chosen to spread their wild.
wedged between the bookends,
loose on the floor, they spill out the door
and down the staircase.
there's a dictionary full of metal spoons,
they belonged to a grandmother of a grandmother
but the hollow book is mine.
there's two small guinea pigs in the corner,
bringing the woodlands into my space,
laughing in the sunlight.
the comforter is covered in trees.
and the salt lamps, well.

they're surprisingly sweet.

so many answers lie in just a drop of compassion;
to be baptized in these waters of empathy
is to move freely upon the earth.
god knows my mind is a place
where curses have come to roost,
but the only times i've known real peace
is when i look through the windows of humanity

and allow my bite to soften.

it is a purple bow
a basket of lilies
a chorus of songbirds,
the weight of their wings.
the flesh of a creature
thought only to exist in myth.

a love like this.

the sky is swaying,
	the trees are still.
her eyes draw the soft red of the curtains
	closed
and come to rest
on the gentler side of my neck.
her fingers trace forest paths
down this earthly skin,
through this fertile land.
the soil is begging to be tilled.
we are desperately ready to cultivate

everything that a mortal life can grow.

the rumours about me span from coast to coast,
ocean to ocean.
humming like a cloud of locusts.
a redbird reputation:
i was struck,
then flame.
combustion; searing orange violence.
but here's the thing;

my backstory doesn't faze her.
much like the heroes in the movies,
i walked out of the explosion
without even turning my head.

all the fire is behind me.

all the smoke has left my lungs.

the premise:

a queer story
in which
the girl holds hands with the other girl
from the start—

because for once,
this version is written

without shame.

representation.

we sit on her bed.
and we sit in her kitchen,
and we host all of the ugliest conversations.
welcoming this growth with open arms
and uncomfortable hearts.
this is the magic of honest communication,
the foundation of sureness we continue to build
cannot be tampered with.

we are in control of our love,
holding each other's hearts so surely—
i could travel the world without worry,
i could walk blindfolded for a thousand days on the edge of the globe,
the steep plunge of nothingness never crossing my mind.
if the world is ending,
she will tell me.
if heaven is afire,
i will let her know.
we'll create an untouchable paradise

incapable of being lost.

the gates of your imagination have always commanded
a stately, pearly sheen.
mine;
touched with brimstone,
but no less elegant.

this is where i reach beyond,
when the light is low enough;
    warm,
    solid.
the calm anticipation joins the sunless sky—
it is here that we may raise poetry from the dead,
lead it home to your hands,
and let the gates close.

until the slumber breaks once more.

i've spent hours
staring through wordless windows
observing a vacant, coastal grey
salt spray that stretches on forever,
much like it's the entirety of this world.

the last time i saw you touch a bird
it lost its song forever.
my back hunched like the wave of this angry sea,
echoing desolation.

it was in this oceanic lament that a moment of clarity struck
with the power of an electric god:
no one will make a songless bird of me again.

your touch was rendered empty as the eyes
that once wandered out the window,

wordless no more.

t'es mon rayon de soleil
she whispers to me,
meaning 'you're my ray of sunshine';
and all i can think while blinking back into her cloudless radiance is

my god baby,

you're the whole damn sky.

i travelled eastward
so i could survive the worst time in my life,
escape the mess that spewed from my loss.
all the while thinking i would be sick with want
for what i left on the west coast.
i lived on the other side of the country,
in the most naturally beautiful city,
for twelve years
thinking it was home—

but what is an ocean
    what is a mountain

without you there to witness it with me?

lay me in the brambles at the foot of an old oak,
in a clearing that only the gods know,
by a river that the stars named after you.
brush that sweet pine smile over my cheek,

and ask me if i hear the waves.

we're filled with vivid emotions, all dressed up in calluses from others.
unwanted parting gifts that just keep giving.
slow, yielding rivers of melancholy slither down the cobblestoned walls of youth.
pooling, and pooling
    into a soft pond at the base of a cliff.
the wise self sees baptism;
    a rebirth.
the truth will shiver out into the cold,
so pristine and raw in its nature,
so worthy to be seen.

make monarchies of your misery.

my lips rest gently on the pulse point of her neck;
the soft swelling of a wave every few seconds.
this is to say
i can kiss her heartbeat

and it's the most honest thing i've tasted in my life.

scented like eden,

hell drips from my teeth.

the day the sea foam spit forth aphrodite,
she waltzed from the waves like a beacon of divinity.
all matter of decay resurrected;
the fruit ripened so deeply,
they spoiled and fell from the branch.
churning the earth below to a sweet, sticky mess.
she was scraped from the sides of the beehive,
so honeyed was her gaze.
the rivers run red as the sullied fruit

and her sweet mouth devours all.

the first day we stepped on the ocean,
she rolled us like dice at a casino;
off kilter, sick in the stomach,
for but a brief moment before striking gold.

each morning, aphrodite rose from her sea bed;
opening her jewelry box to the horizon,
and the water glimmered like a million lighters in a crowd.
like the music had just begun to swell.

blood flows different under spanish moons;
we stand vigilant and watch
past lives melt like cotton candy into the blue.

i once found myself lost at sea,
but what i discovered out there was as reassuring,
as steady as a lone jack pine,
centered on a glittering canadian landscape:

life's oceans are full of strong, ebbing seafoam tides;

and they will always pull me home.

acknowledgments

to my mom, my on-call editor and the first one to like all my Instagram posts: thank you for always believing in me. i promise that someday i will learn the proper use of the apostrophe.

to my dad, who only started reading poetry when i started writing it. thanks for dropping everything to fly to wherever i am when i need you.

to my grandmothers for being the twin pillars of my creation, for their wisdom, their love, and their magic.

to my brother mac, who helped me write the letter to central avenue about publishing this book. thank you for the ideas and support, the many teas you bought me, and for making your friends order my books.

to my cousin anna, my personal social media consultant, for helping me promote my work and preventing me from using too many filters on tiktok.

to michelle at central avenue publishing for taking a chance on me, to beau for your editing insight and craft, and the wonderful team who made this project into more than i could have all on my own. thank you for the art within the pages, for the belief in my poems, for your ideas and perspectives. thank you to molly for your keen eye and thorough proofread.

to each pen that made my handwriting loop extra nicely, or that formed the words even when my hands were shaking or the ink blurred.

and thank you to every circumstance of my life that led each river of my being to the unconditional ocean of love that it is to be with my partner, chantal.

alannah radburn, her partner, and her guinea pigs live in québec, just over the bridge from her hometown of ottawa. she is currently far from the ebbing tides of the pacific, where she started writing this book, but is always immersed in the sea of life's emotions. follow her on instagram and tiktok for more posts, poems, and whimsy.

@alannahradburn.poetry